Ten P
about ~~~w

ex libris

Candlestick Press

Published by:
Candlestick Press,
Diversity House, 72 Nottingham Road, Arnold, Nottingham NG5 6LF
www.candlestickpress.co.uk

Design and typesetting by Craig Twigg

Printed by Ratcliff & Roper Print Group, Nottinghamshire, UK

Cover illustration © Sam Cannon, 2019
www.samcannonart.co.uk

Candlestick Press monogram © Barbara Shaw, 2008

© Candlestick Press, 2019

Donation to Shelter
www.shelter.org.uk

ISBN 978 1 907598 84 5

Acknowledgements:

The poems in this pamphlet are reprinted from the following books, all by
permission of the publishers listed unless stated otherwise. Every effort has
been made to trace the copyright holders of the poems published in this book.
The editor and publisher apologise if any material has been included without
permission or without the appropriate acknowledgement, and would be glad to be
told of anyone who has not been consulted.

Thanks are due to all the copyright holders cited below for their kind permission:

Carole Bromley, poem first published in this pamphlet. Billy Collins, *Picnic,
Lightning* (University of Pittsburgh Press, 1998). Kerry Darbishire, poem first
published in this pamphlet. Lucy Jeynes, poem first published in this pamphlet.
Joanne Key, poem first published in this pamphlet. Gill McEvoy, poem first
published in this pamphlet. Jill Munro, poem first published in this pamphlet.
Meda AA Stamper, poem first published in this pamphlet. CK Williams,
Collected Poems (Bloodaxe Books, 2006) www.bloodaxebooks.com

All permissions cleared courtesy of Swift Permissions
(swiftpermissions@gmail.com).

Where poets are no longer living, their dates are given.

Introduction

Poets have long been inspired by snow. It transforms the world, however fleetingly. It brings out the child in all of us. It can be inconvenient, dangerous, even lethal.

In response to our snow poem competition, poems came in from all over the world about all aspects of snow: snow globes, snow angels, snowmen, sledging. There were also beautiful poems about everything from wedding days to losing loved ones, from the way snow arrives unexpectedly to the way it lingers in the hedges. In the end, I chose three winners and three runners-up, all of which are here. The winning poems by Lucy Jeynes, Joanne Key and Meda Stamper are all characterised by a vividly emotional response and each has its own particular beauty.

These poets join writers from Robert Frost to contemporary voices such as Billy Collins and CK Williams. Collins invites us to see the snow which falls "so indifferently/into the spacious white parlor of the world" where he is listening to music, while CK Williams gives us a vivid memory of his lover walking away in the snow eating a red apple while "the first/delighted children rushed out with sleds".

Elsewhere, we find everything from Wordsworth skating in his black coat to a childhood memory of being cast as a snowflake, from Dr Zhivago writing poems with ice on his moustache to an adult wishing she had paused to catch snowflakes on her tongue.

Snow then, from waking to its magic in the early morning to watching it fall at dusk on woods that are "lovely, dark, and deep". Enjoy every flake.

Carole Bromley

The Star of Bethlehem

I longed to be a Virgin Mary,
innkeeper's wife or angel
but was cast a snowflake –
a small Spirograph of sharp
elbows and pointy knees.

My mother slashed a sheet –
not quite white enough for her bed –
cut sleeve-holes to make me sleet,
roughly glued on cotton wool puffs,
made a head-hole for the snow-ghost of me.

My role – to drift in lightly, *pianissimo* –
dance a snowfall, bank myself along
with all the other fake flakes,
form a snow blanket on the scene –
chill the gym floor to a Nazareth road.

Jill Munro

Snow Day

One cubic foot of snow contains a billion snowflakes.
Each one is unique.

It snowed in the night – we woke to
A muffling quiet and absence of cars
Bright grey light at the crack of the curtains
The pristine eiderdown of lawn
Scrimshawed with footprints of a mouse
Then we sighed, found boots in the cellar
Scraped the windscreen, warmed the engine
Went to work like any other morning.

We did not jump in the deepest drift
Roll handfuls for a snowball fight
We did not go sledging, make snow angels
We did not build a snowman with rakish hat,
A cheery crooked carrot for his nose
Or shake it from low branches like glitter.
It was February, only to be expected
An inconvenient start, a busy day.

By teatime it was greasy slush
Splashing the kerb, ruining shoes
Patches at the ankles of the hedge
All washed away by morning.
There is a last time for everything
As life tips past the half-way mark
I should have stopped to bear witness:
Caught snowflakes on my tongue.

Lucy Jeynes

According to Met Office records, the last snow fell in England on
6 February 2025.

Snow: II

It's very cold, Catherine is bundled in a coat, a poncho on top of that,
    high boots, gloves,
a long scarf around her neck, and she's sauntering up the middle of the
    snowed-in street,
eating, of all things, an apple, the blazing redness of which shocks
    against the world of white.
No traffic yet, the *crisp crisp* of her footsteps keeps reaching me until she
    turns the corner.
I write it down years later, and the picture still holds perfectly, precise,
    unwanting,
and so too does the sense of being suddenly bereft as she passes abruptly
    from my sight,
the quick wash of desolation, the release again into the memory of affec-
    tion, and then affection,
as the first trucks blundered past, chains pounding, the first delighted
    children rushed out with sleds.

CK Williams (1936 – 2015)

The Symmetry of Snow

Maybe Shakespeare is right that mercy is like dew
But grace is surely snow, falling in the early morning, like a
    second chance –
Or whichever chance I'm on now (I've lost count) – while it is
    still dark
Snow is what grace is like, falling in every symmetrical flake
Every flake symmetrical – even though you know this only if
    you enlarge it
Beyond what the eye can see – beauty down deep
Grace is not there to impress you
Snow isn't for your sake either
Snow has its own reasons, like grace
It cannot help falling

Maybe mercy falls like gentle dew invisible
But grace shows its heart like snow and changes everything
Everything even what we've made all wrong and ugly
Everything is all the same in beauty after snow
Asphalt is the color of earth and grass
Because snow is the great equalizer

It also cools and if you have a fever it could save you
But if you are cold already with no warm place to nestle
No window at which to stand inside and watch
Then snow is not like grace
The bird I heard singing just now is
The bird singing in the cold dark early – alone she was
A soloist in down – but now the others have started
In the early morning, which I see now isn't dark any more
When I turned away it grew the pale grey blue of early day
The birdsong did it – that is what grace is like
If you have no warm place or built-in down on a snowy morning
    before dawn
No space heater to switch on or warm bed to climb back into
Then snowfall isn't like grace, no matter how symmetrical in
    deep-down beauty

Because even symmetrically cold can do you in
Then grace isn't snow at all – it is the birdsong
Which while you're listening to it
Day breaks

But if you have a warm spot or your own down or fur or blubber
    built in or a high fever
Then what I said before is true: Snow – like the snowfall I saw
    this morning
As you walked down the steps and drove away
And I stood at the window and held the cat warm and purring
Heart to heart with me as we watched the snow fall –
That is like grace, making all things new
In the very early morning while it is still dark

Now it is pale violet blue where it was grey moments ago
When that first bird made the light
And the snow has stopped – looking out the window from my bed
I think it is already melting or didn't stick to some trees at all –
But for that brief time there were second chances on offer
And I was given one without doing anything but stand and watch
And feel the cat's warm heartbeat and hear the bird
While grace fell silently with symmetry I could not see
Because grace just is, like snow
Even if I had not seen it fall at all

Meda AA Stamper

When it Snowed

you made it sound simple:
how wild geese flying south

over Grizedale forest is a sign,
how ice used to paralyse Esthwaite lake

where Wordsworth skated
in his black coat, how winters fall

like prayers, how snow stitches
and mends all that is broken.

Through the pale hospital window
I watch roofs blanket white, cars

balancing great hats, footprints healing
themselves as if to trick me into believing

it's just another of your winter days
and everything will recover.

Kerry Darbishire

St Valentine's Day, 1969

Today is our wedding day and overnight
in this sleepless city, Dublin, it has snowed.

Today the world is white – whiter, purer than the dress
that hangs beside my bed in readiness.

The fabric of my gown is cold,
my breath hangs white on threads of air.

Beyond ice-patterned glass the garden
wears a wedding veil of snow.

I race outside to make my mark on it
placing my bare feet down in its melting chill,

As if somehow I can print this day into Eternity,
hold it in my mind forever so:
delight, and snow.

Gill McEvoy

for the love of snow

tonight the sky is full
    of us
        my blank page
your stark light
    thank heavens
for clean slates
    of silence
and absence

  flakes
    of you
        begin
            to fall
  I'll wait
as long as it takes
    and start small
    bring your old scarf
from the back of the wardrobe
    make a heart
        from a snow ball
    soon enough
you're standing in front of me
        with that same old smile
    a new man
made of all that is pure and driven
        reformed
as always   as always
    forgiven

Joanne Key

Snow

after Don Paterson

I hate all films that start with snow,
Christmas schmaltz the lot of them:
Bambi, Love Story, Frozen.

The cynical director, his assistant
with the snow machine
blowing fluffy cotton-wool flakes

to muffle the cries of motherless fawn,
orphaned little girls in castles,
a young wife breathing her last.

I've nothing against a good cry
and I'll make an exception
for *Doctor Zhivago* and the ice palace

where Yuri will make a fresh start
despite the wolves, will write poems
in fingerless gloves, ice on his moustache,

even though I know it won't end well,
that she'll step into the fur-lined sleigh,
that he'll breathe a hole in the ice for one last look.

Carole Bromley

Snow

I cannot help noticing how this slow Monk solo
seems to go somehow
with the snow
that is coming down this morning,

how the notes and the spaces accompany
its easy falling
on the geometry of the ground,
on the flagstone path,
the slanted roof,
and the angles of the split rail fence

as if he had imagined a winter scene
as he sat at the piano
late one night at the Five Spot
playing 'Ruby My Dear.'

Then again, it's the kind of song
that would go easily with rain
or a tumult of leaves,

and for that matter it's a snow
that could attend
an adagio for strings,
the best of the Ronettes,
or George Thorogood and the Destroyers.

It falls so indifferently
into the spacious white parlor of the world,
if I were sitting here reading
in silence,

reading the morning paper
or reading *Being and Nothingness*
not even letting the spoon
touch the inside of the cup,
I have a feeling
the snow would even go perfectly with that.

Billy Collins

Stopping by Woods on a Snowy Evening

Whose woods these are I think I know.
His house is in the village, though;
He will not see me stopping here
To watch his woods fill up with snow.

My little horse must think it queer
To stop without a farmhouse near
Between the woods and frozen lake
The darkest evening of the year.

He gives his harness bells a shake
To ask if there is some mistake.
The only other sound's the sweep
Of easy wind and downy flake.

The woods are lovely, dark, and deep,
But I have promises to keep,
And miles to go before I sleep,
And miles to go before I sleep.

Robert Frost (1874 – 1963)